From a Peasant to a Princess

From a Peasant to a Princess

An Orphan's Guide to Healing, Restoration and Wholeness

By
Kim Hood

E-BookTime, LLC
Montgomery, Alabama

From a Peasant to a Princess
An Orphan's Guide to Healing, Restoration and Wholeness

Copyright © 2006 by Kim Hood

All rights reserved. No part of this book may be reproduced or transmitted in any form or by any means, electronic or mechanical, including photocopying, recording, or by any information storage and retrieval system, without permission in writing from the copyright owner.

Library of Congress Control Number: 2006931916

ISBN: 1-59824-321-7

First Edition
Published August 2006
E-BookTime, LLC
6598 Pumpkin Road
Montgomery, AL 36108
www.e-booktime.com

Dedication

This book is dedicated to each orphan, foster, and adoptive child who struggles to find his or her place in this world due to abuse, abandonment or the death of biological parents.

Contents

Acknowledgments 9

Introduction *Open Arms* 11

Chapter One *Why Do Abusers Abuse?* 17

Chapter Two *Abandoned!* 25

Chapter Three *A Roof Over My Head Is Not Enough!* 31

Chapter Four *I Do Not Want To Be Insecure!* 43

Chapter Five *Anger!* 51

Chapter Six *Fourteen Going on Twenty-Four!* 55

Chapter Seven *A Home for the Holidays?* 61

Chapter Eight *You Can Make It!* 67

EL Corizon de la Princesa 75

Scriptures 76

Notes 77

Sources 81

Acknowledgments

To my loving Heavenly Father: "Thanks" for keeping your promises to me. I appreciate your loving arms that continue to shield me from the enemy. You cared for me often when I did not care about myself. It did not matter what was going on in my life you let me know that I am important to you, so for that, I say, "Thank you! Thanks for your love and for giving me hope and a future."

To my greatest inspiration, my mother Betty, who always believed in me, encouraged me and inspired me to be my best. Although she was taken way too soon, her love, inspiration, and encouragement will live on forever in my heart.

To Willie, my dad, AKA "soldier boy" who was a mighty man of valor: Thanks for the solid foundation you provided and the love you shared you with us. You will always be a special part of my life.

Open Arms

Life is a journey and each of us travels a singular and oftentimes uncertain path. Our journey as we know it begins sheltered in our mother's womb. Anxiousness, excitement, and relief fill the room as the doctor yells "Push!" One more big push and before you know it, a new life has begun. With cries of joy, baby proclaims, "I am here!" At this time, the newborn no longer has the shelter and security of its mother's womb. Baby must now begin to grow and experience life first hand.

We can definitely conclude that it does not matter what stage you are in on life's journey, sometimes life can be scary. Life's changing seasons offer unique challenges. Christ is very aware of the various challenges and seasons we must go through. In his eminent wisdom he has provided relief, encouragement, and strength for us to walk in victory on our life's journey. **ISAIAH chapter 61 verses 1 and 2** says, **"The sprit of the Lord God is upon me; because the Lord hath anointed me to preach good tidings unto the meek: He hath sent me to bind up the broken hearted, to proclaim liberty to the captives, and the opening of the prison doors to them that are bound; to proclaim the acceptable year of the lord, and the day of vengeance of our God; to comfort all that mourn."**

That reminds me of one of my favorite stories: Frank Braum's "The Wonderful Wizard of Oz." Motown produced a spectacular musical based on this Broadway production entitled "The Wiz". In the "Wiz" Dorothy begins a journey that is predestined for her. **Ephesians 1:4-5** says, **"According as he hath chosen us in him before the foundation of the world, that we should be holy and without blame before him in love: Having predestined us unto**

Introduction

the adoption of children by Jesus Christ himself, according to the good pleasure of his will." Plainly stated, God chose us from the foundation of the world and he has a wonderful destiny for us. Let us look at: **Jeremiah 29:11** as it says: **"For I know the thoughts that I think toward you says the Lord, thoughts of peace, and not of evil, to give you an expected end."** Now I am not suggesting that God predestined the character Dorothy's steps in the actual musical, since it is a fictitious play. However, I am pointing out that just as Dorothy had to travel down the yellow brick road in search of a supreme being -- "The Wiz" -- she was required to help someone along her way. Dorothy discovered that as she helped the seemingly brainless scarecrow, the seemingly heartless tin man and the seemingly cowardly lion, not only was she able to help her friends realize their gifts and talents; but she also realized hers as well. Therefore, as Dorothy sought to return home to a physical location, Glenda the good witch kindly pointed out that "Home is a place we all must find within ourselves. Child, it's knowing your mind; it's knowing your heart, and knowing your courage." She went on to say (paraphrase) that if we know ourselves that we are always home no matter where we are.

This reminds me of Joseph, the Prince of Egypt. This young man seemed to experience at an early age devastation after devastation, nevertheless the Lord was with Joseph. Primarily, we know Rachel, his mother died giving birth to Benjamin, his younger brother. Secondly, we know that Joseph was hated by his brethren, attacked by his brethren, and then put into a pit to die. However, instead of dying in the pit, he was sold into slavery and consequently separated from his earthly father **Genesis Chapter 34 and verse 4** explains: **"And when his brethren saw that their father loved him more than all his brethren, they hated him, and could not speak peaceably unto him."** Wow! What a way to begin this journey called life! Let us see what happens next to Joseph. **Genesis 37:20** goes on to explain the dastardly plan that Joseph's brothers hatched: **"Come now therefore and let us slay him, and cast him into some pit, and we will say some evil beast hath devoured him: and we shall see what becomes of his dreams."** Verses 24 through 27 tell us, **"And they took and cast**

Introduction

him into a pit: and the pit was empty, there was no water in it: and they sat down to eat bread: And they lifted up their eyes and looked, and beheld a company of Ishmaelite came from Gilead with their camels bearing spices and balm and myrrh, going to carry it down to Egypt. And Judah said unto his brethren, 'What profit is it if we slay our brother, and conceal his blood? Come, let us sell him to the Ishmaelite, and let not our hand be upon him: For he is our brother and our flesh. And his brethren were content."** Please be advised that although these injustices would seem to be enough, however, there is more. When we read **Genesis, Chapter 39**, we see that Joseph was placed into the home of Potiphar, an officer of Egypt. Verses 6 and 7 say, **"and he left all that he had in Joseph's hand: And he knew not aught he had save the bread which he did eat. And Joseph was a goodly person, and well favored. And it came to pass after these things, that his master's wife cast her eyes upon Joseph: And she said, 'Lie with me.'"** Well Joseph refused but was accused of this wrong doing anyway. Joseph was put in prison. However, the favor of God was upon Joseph's life -- so much so, that it did not matter what situation Joseph found himself in, he prospered. Verse 21 explains: **"But the Lord was with Joseph, and showed him mercy, and gave him favor in the sight of the keeper of the prison."**

We know that wrongful imprisonment was not Joseph's dwelling place. God had much more in store for Joseph. We know this because of the gift of interpreting dreams that God placed in Joseph. Joseph was able to solve a problem for the Governor of Egypt by interpreting his dream. Joseph's reward was an appointment second in command to Pharaoh to rule over all of the land of Egypt. Wow! Is not that great news? Take heart, my friend, and know that God will not forget about you; the Lord will be with you wherever your journey in life takes you. Just think; even when the world has mistreated and abused you, the Lord will never leave, forsake, nor abandon you. He will in his timing bring deliverance to your situation, just as he did Joseph's. We find that Joseph was eventually reunited with his earthly father Jacob and reconciled to his brothers. God is so good that the same brothers who sought to

Introduction

kill Joseph had to rely on him for food in the famine. The irony of the situation is Joseph's brethren who initially thought to kill him, had to rely on him for "Life" because if he had not fed them, they would have perished in the famine. God blessed Joseph to not only prosper finally, but to also have an understanding and forgiveness toward his brethren regarding his life and the direction God chose for him. Joseph explained this to his brothers: **Genesis chapter 45: v 5** states: **"Now therefore be not grieved, nor angry with yourselves, that ye sold me hither: For God did send me before you to preserve life."** We also see in chapter 50 verse 20 that Joseph acknowledges the wrongdoing of his brethren by declaring: **"But as for you, ye thought evil against me: But God meant it unto my good, to bring to pass, as it is this day, to save much people alive."**

Today we have assurance through Christ Jesus that our loving heavenly father loves us in the same manner, if not greater. We know that he sent his son Jesus to die for us. Jesus still stands with open arms to give us a home in him on earth as well as in heaven. For you see until we accept Christ and his love, we are his prodigal sons and daughters who asked for our inheritance, left home and squandered or wasted it. Upon our return to Christ, he will greet us with open arms just like the father did when the prodigal son returned home. The Gospel according to **Luke, Chapter 15: v. 18-20** says: **"I will arise and go to my father, and will say unto him, "Father, I have sinned against the heaven and before thee. And I am no more worthy to be called thy son: Make me as one of thy hired servants. And he arose, and came to his father. But when he was yet a great way off, his father saw him and had compassion, and ran, and fell on his neck and kissed him."** As you read this book please allow the Holy Spirit to minister to your innermost being, touching the broken places that, perhaps, you did not even know existed.

This book is birthed through the struggles I faced and overcame as an orphan and foster child. I hope, for those of you who are orphans, that this book will encourage you and let you know that with God as your father, you can be successful. Furthermore,

Introduction

despite the struggles you will face in life, you are victorious. May God's peace, love, and comfort heal you every where you hurt.

In the year two-thousand and three an estimated three million cases of child abuse and neglect were reported according to the Child Welfare League of America.

Chapter One

Why Do Abusers Abuse?

This chapter initially poses a question that engenders much philosophical, sociological and psychological debate. Why do abusers abuse? In my attempt to answer that question, I have first tried to define abuse. Abuse often occurs in many forms but can be simply described as an attitude or behavior that results in harming another individual. The harm can be physical, verbal, emotional, or sexual in nature. In our ideal world we would not typically think of being abused by friends or loved ones. However, in reality the fact is we all have abused or mistreated someone at some point in our lives. Most people do not want to think of themselves as acting in an abusive manner toward another. However, sometimes we have mistreated others, whether it was unintentional or on purpose. As an example, think about the husband who ignores the request of his wife for several weeks to spend quality time with her. He suggests that it is due to the daunting project he must complete at work. Yet, he manages to find time to play golf with friends each week faithfully. This is emotional abuse, as it will almost surely send a message to the patient wife that golf is more important than spending time with her. Or, let us look at the parent who chooses to respond inappropriately to his son, who struggled at a tee ball game by striking out on the first bat and getting put out on the second hit. When asked how did I do at the baseball game today dad? Dad responds in an abusive manner by yelling, "That was the sorriest game I ever saw! You can't hit the ball; you can't run. You play like a sissy!" Such behavior conveys a message to the child that even though I did my very best, that is not good enough for dad and I am not accepted by him. This type of abuse is primarily verbal abuse. I say primarily because often when one type of abuse is present the other types exist as well. For example, the mother who blames her daughter for her own inability to maintain a relationship with a man. In anger, she slaps and burns her daughter with a cigarette, then locks her in a closet every Saturday. This is one form of physical abuse. Such abuse is definitely modeling to the young child that it's ok to blame and act in violence, when things do not go our way. The worst message given in this scenario is that the mother's relationship with a man is far more important than the relationship with her daughter.

Now, I think the most sensitive type of abuse is known as sexual abuse. Sexual abuse can range from inappropriate staring and glaring to full-fledged sexual indiscretions. Let us look at the step-dad who is confused in his thinking and abusive in his actions as he expresses it through inappropriate behaviors such as manipulations, fondling, and perhaps intercourse with his step child (male or female). Inappropriate learned sexual behaviors and emotional scars are among the sad consequences of such abuse. These are all examples blatant abuse. If you are reading this book and are currently in an abusive situation please take the following steps to help yourself. Primarily take courage and strength in the bosom of Jesus **Psalm 28 verse 7** states it this way **"The lord is my strength and my shield; my heart trusted in him, and I am helped; therefore my heart greatly rejoiceth; and with my song will I praise him."** Secondarily, confide in a teacher or counselor you trust and ask for their assistance to report abuse the authorities or police. No matter what age you are, this can be a scary step but you matter to your heavenly father, you re important to him. **Psalm 55:18** says, **"He hath delivered my soul in peace from the battle that was against me; for there were many with me."** Please know the civil and public servant system was established a long time ago to intervene and bring justice to circumstances and people who violate the law. Although there are no perfect entities in existence today, if God be for you, who can be against you? Therefore, please know that you matter as well as your safety.

From a Peasant to a Princess

I think it is beneficial for me to point out that sometimes until a person discovers how much our heavenly fathers values and loves them, they are unable to recognize that they do not deserve to be abused or mistreated (regardless of the excuses offered by the abuser). Emotional abuse and verbal abuses are the least recognizable types of abuse. When one is not whole, that person may be more susceptible to feelings like: I deserve to be treated badly. I am not worthy to be loved, because my mother or father left me. Or, that person may feel that he or she has no choice but to tolerate the abuse because no one will believe or help them. Furthermore, feelings of embarrassment, helplessness, and loneliness often cloud our being. It is not until a kind word or a revelation is provided that we realize that this abuse is not normal. We realize that we should be treated in a better manner. It is then we begin to grasp the concept and knowledge that God loves us and has so much more for us in life.

Earlier in the chapter I attempted to define abuse and its common types. However, let us look at the subtle ways in which maltreatment and abuse sometimes can occur in various types of foster care. When I say foster care or home, one might typically think of a court-ordered placement in a state certified foster home or residential treatment center. However, I am not limiting my definition to only placements monitored by a state or adoption agency. I would also like to include the countless number of children and teens who never enter into the legal system for assistance with their living upon separation from their parents; either through death, abuse, or abandonment. I am sure you will agree with me that it is such a blessing to have a relative or friend, who is loving and responsible enough to take the initiative and care for a child that is not there own. By definition, these children are considered to be in relative placements.

One of my purposes for writing this book is simply to offer a ray of hope and encouragement for children and adults alike who have experienced low self esteem among other challenges while growing up without the emotional support of their biological parents, or perhaps anyone. The points of view presented are real occurrences and are taken from *my* perspectives and experiences.

Additionally, this book is designed to minister to readers of all ages. Therefore, some of the terminology I chose to use may not be that of an official state entity or government agency, but rather my chose to define as I discuss topics on a basic level that are easy to understand for most readers. Furthermore, there are *numerous* state and adoption agencies who place children who are abused and neglected. Each agency have there *own* set of expectations, qualifications, and services they provide to their clientele. Therefore, this book does not represent any specific agency but rather provides a general overview of interactions of which I have experienced. (Now! -- I have gotten my disclaimer out of the way let's allow the Holy Spirit to proceed.)

Let's start by looking at King David in the Book of Psalms as it appears he has to face many disheartening situations. But we find specifically, in **Psalm 27:10**, he declares **"When my mother and my father forsook me, then, the Lord will take me up."** This promise is a light in the mist of darkness to anyone who have ever faced the trauma of losing their parents, whether it's to death, divorce, and/or abandonment. David realized the importance of relying on God for his source of guidance, comfort, and correction. Our heavenly father will often place people in our lives to help mentor us and coach us along our way. Every situation we find ourselves in is an opportunity for spiritual growth and personal development. What matters is simply the attitude we take when we face injustice and unpleasant situations in our lives. David, although anointed to be king, had the very unpleasant experience of sitting under a mentor who was jealous of him and as a result of that jealousy; he had to daily face life threatening encounters while maintaining an attitude acceptable to God. Now initially, King Saul was not bitter towards David. **I Samuel chapter eighteen verse 5** explains: **"and David went out whithersoever Saul sent him, and behaved himself wisely: and Saul set him over the men of war, and he was accepted in the sight of all the people, and also in the sight of Saul servant's. But King Saul recognized the anointing upon David's life and began to see that the people were beginning to cater to David more than him. Therefore, he became jealous and bitter towards David so much so he wanted** him dead." Let us look at chapter 19 verse 1: **"and Saul, spake to Jonathan his son, and to all his servants, that they should kill David."** With that said, we see that even though it's always God's intention to bless and prosper us, sometimes others may enter our lives with the best of intentions to help and encourage us, but sometimes it does not always turn out for the best.

For example, let's look at the individual who initially may foster children as a good deed or through a since of family obligation but later find themselves caring for the child(ren) in a resentful, hurtful and emotionally traumatic way. Perhaps the abuse or maltreatment is due to the abuse the caregiver once experienced, or perhaps they now view that child as an unnecessary burden that robs them of time and resources for themselves or their nuclear family.

In order for one to be successful where they are, they must understand where they have been. If you have an understanding of where you have been so to speak, you are now equipped with the tools needed to better prepare you for your future. In terms of family traits and blood lines, we know that we often shared both positive and negative traits of family members. From a biblical perspective, we know the bible refers to familiar sins and transgressions; (Negative habits and strong holds) that may show-up in our family blood line, up to the third or forth generation or a generation curse as it is commonly known. Let's say that if one's great grandmother, LuAnn developed a habit of drinking alcohol to cope with her stresses of life. More than likely her daughter (grandmother) will have the predisposition (favorable conditions for use as a result of learned behaviors) for her to also abuse alcohol as a way to cope with her stresses of life, as well. Additionally, please note generation curses are not limited to every generation. It is important to note that sometimes they actually skip a generation or change its form of the addictive behavior. For example, in the situation above, we see that great grandmother LuAnn, abused alcohol to cope, well her daughter, Louise may smoke cigarettes and not consume alcohol at all. Now we are up to the current generation, let's say Louise's daughter, Lisa is acutely aware of the negative effects of smoking and drinking on the mind and body and is able to effectively cope without either substance. However, she seems to always date men with alcohol addictions. Can you see the cycle? Jesus is well aware of this cycle and offers the following solution in **Matthew 11:28-30: "Come unto me all that labor and are heavy laden, and I will give you rest. Take my yoke upon you, and learn of me; for I am meek and lowly in heart. For my yoke is easy, and my burden is light."** You see you do not have to be caught up in a cycle of abuse as an abuser or as the one who is abused. Simply allow the love of God to transform your life one day at a time.

I was blessed to eventually be reared in a loving caring Godly Christian home, after the death of my mother. However, I did have my share of challenges in this and other areas of my life. It is by God's mercy, grace, and love I was able to overcome. Since God allowed me to overcome I can minister to you through first hand experiences. Additionally, I have had the privilege of working with children in many capacities including both long term and short term foster home placements, as well as residential treatment centers and private relative placements. I have also worked with at risk girls as a big sister and CASA volunteer. It is through these past experiences I have found most adoption and foster care agencies as well as state agencies do a remarkable job in terms of providing services to meet the child's financial needs. However what about personal relative placements? What about the children who are recipients of their inheritance or death survivor benefits? These are private entities where it is possible that the parents or guardian does not have to give accountability to anyone. Will the funds designated for the care of the children be used for the care of the children? Later on I will look at this a little more in depth. However, for now, do you remember an extreme case of financial neglect and abuse in a foster home which gained national media attention some years ago? Do you recall the foster children who slept in cages at night and, according to the media, lived in a decrepit old home? These conditions existed even though the foster parents reportedly received thousands of dollars a month for the care of the children. Meanwhile, less severe cases may occur every day that never make media attention. As you keep reading, you will encounter more revelation on this topic. But for now, I will simply say child care reimbursements, inheritances and death survivor death benefits are provided for the foster child(ren's) welfare and when it is not used for that purpose, the child(ren) are victimized again. Please note not only does that negatively impact the child(ren) but is theft, as well and it would seem that the Lord is not pleased with this type of behavior. According to scripture he says this about his children. **Matthew chapter eighteen verses 6 and 7** explains **"and whoso shall receive one such little child in my name recieveth me. But whoso shall offend one of these little ones which believe in me, it were better for him that a millstone were hanged about his neck, and were drowned in the depth of the sea."**

Later we will discuss the emotional scars and other types of subtle abuses. Be encouraged as you read on and keep an open heart to the healing power of the Holy Spirit. Help is on the way!

According to the US Department of Health and Human Services, as of April Two Thousand and Five, Five Hundred Twenty-Three Thousand and Eighty-Five children were in foster care.

Chapter Two

Abandoned!

There are many forms of abandonment; no one typical definition will suffice. However, you will notice throughout this book that I often refer back to issues that stem from abandonment, with regard to the parent child relationship. I intentionally continued that theme to express the severity of the trauma caused when children are abandoned by their biological parents. Most children who are in foster care and who have a guardian(s) have had their biological parents in their life at some point and time. However, maybe due to their death, as it was in my case, they were abandoned by them. Please do not misunderstand this example; for we know that death is a normal part of the life process. Let us take a look at **Hebrews Chapter 9: v 27** as it states **"And as it is appointed unto men once to die, but after this the judgment."** However, it does not make the pain of losing your parents any less painful. Likewise, maybe you lost your biological parents, because they decided it would be better for you to be adopted and you were placed in the "system" until you were adopted. Finally, you may fit the category of thousands of children who were removed from their biological parents because of abuse or neglect inflicted by them. Whatever the reason is that you have found yourself in the care of a guardian or foster parent; you can acknowledge that there are probably issues you must deal with in order to have a healthy relationship with others. Sometimes, crippling emotional issues exist (we are not always aware of what they are) that limit us in our growth and success in life. When we do not deal with our issues, we learn to put up walls to protect ourselves from others who may potentially hurt us. Ideally, this is great; but the same wall we put up to protect us may also keep those out who are trying to help us. Therefore, it is in our best interest to deal with abandonment issues, forgive, and allow the Holy Spirit to heal us.

Please note that, depending upon your circumstance, you may be actually blessed in life to find or develop a relationship with your biological parent(s). You may have the opportunity to have every question answered that have plagued your being for years. Well, what are you going to do with this information? Will your heart be in a place to receive the information and forgive those who have hurt you? If you find that this will be a challenge for you, please keep reading. By the time you finish this book, you will know that all of God's best is available to you now.

Down through the years, even before I was born, there has been one sure fire way to have a hit record. I say that because since the beginning of time, society has sung different songs with a familiar theme that evolves around the fear of being alone. From the popular '70's tune sung by Eric Carmen entitled *"All by Myself"* to Michael Jackson's *"You are not Alone"*, we have embraced the need to love and be loved by someone. We have an underlying fear of going through life alone. Some of us at adult age are better able to deal with the challenges of life without the support of a significant other in form of parents or spouse etc. But for others, at whatever age, the fear of being alone is so gripping that at the very threat of someone leaving their life, whether it's verbal or implied may imprison that person. And it is at this point, they may be willing to subject themselves to their abuser and please them at the cost of sacrificing themselves, their happiness and well being, simply to avoid being alone. Jesus offered a remedy for the state of being alone in that he said, "I will never leave or forsake you!"

Oftentimes, we misunderstand the state of being alone for the state of being lonely. The two are very different. A simple definition for alone is "without another person present." On the contrary, lonely is defined as "feeling deserted or depressed because of a lack of companionship." The differentiating term seems to be "feeling." It is quite possible to live a full life, content without the presence of another in terms of friends, parents, or spouse. However, God designed us to have fellowship with one another. He established this primarily in the family unit. (See chapter on marriage). Therefore, if you find yourself without another person (single) to assist you on your journey in this particular season of your life, keep a good attitude and try to avoid "Stinking Thinking". Negative or ill thinking on a consistent basis may only lead to feelings of depression and anxiety. Be patient with yourself and with God; you will discover later that "to everything there is a season." Your troubles will not last always!

Now let us look at some negative attributes commonly associated with loneliness-- clingy, fearful, and possessive, are familiar terms that often describe some lonely people. I am sure we all know someone who has exhibited clingy, fearful or possessive behaviors; maybe even we ourselves have been! I'm sure you're familiar with the example of the three year old who has a birthday party. While at the party, his four year old friend grabs a truck that has not been touched in a year. Then all of a sudden, the three year old develops an intense interest in that truck.

Or perhaps, you are dating the high school football jock who is so controlling and feels threatened if you, literally talk to another guy. So he tells you, his sweety not tot talk, chum, or partner up in biology class with any guy. I cannot forget the wife who allows herself to suffer physical abuse by the hand of her husband because she is fearful of living without him. Perhaps, her fear may be due to the lack of finances among other important reasons.

Please keep in mind on your journey to healing and being made whole that the Lord places people in our lives for a season. While we are in our season we should maximize our potential by cherishing the people he has placed in our lives and the time we are allowed to have with them. Ironically, when the plan of God calls for us to separate ourselves or maybe not have as much contact as we once had with those people, due to personal or spiritual growth. We should be encouraged to let go of those people and their relationship. When God instructs us to move on and let them go. Remember, the Word of God says in **Romans 1:17: "Every good and perfect gift is**

from above, and cometh down from the father of lights, with whom there is no variableness, neither shadow of turning." This basically indicates our heavenly father knows what is best for us. Let me say it as CO-Pastor Paula White of Without Walls Church would: "The Lord sends people into our lives to bless us but the devil sends people in our lives to hurt us." The Book of **John 10:10** confirms that very fact, as Jesus declares **"The thief cometh not, but for to steal, and to kill, and to destroy. I am come that they might have life, and that they might have it more abundantly."** Is not that exciting to know that our heavenly father has a better plan for your life. Please know that inspite of who enters the door of your heart or who exits the door of your heart, you can take comfort in knowing that Jesus is standing at the door of your heart, knocking desiring to come in! Will you open the door to your heart and let him in?

Fifty-seven point one percent of abused and neglected children in Two Thousand and Three received follow-up services according to the US Department of Health and Human Services.

Chapter Three

A Roof Over My Head Is Not Enough!

The ministry of foster parenting, regardless of how we define foster parents -- relative, guardian, or actual state appointed foster parent, -- is exactly that: a ministry. The Bible in the Book of **Ephesians chapter 6 verse 4** has this to say about parents and there role(s): **"And, ye fathers, provoke not your children to wrath: but bring them up in the nurture and admonition of the Lord."** This is an important fact in the parent/child relationship, as it should be the mindset or basis of the relationship. If every person who has accepted the challenge to minister to orphans and abused/neglected children would embrace "the ministry mindset," then good seeds would spring up and develop in the child's life. Seeds as we know grow and bloom into a harvest. Therefore, the type of harvest you desire is based upon the type of seed you choose to sow today. For example, if you want others to be patient with you, then you should take the initiative and sow patience into the lives of others. If you desire mercy in your life, then sow mercy it will come back to you. Where, when, and through whom your seed returns unto you is not at your discretion. In fact **Ecclesiastics 11:16** says **"Cast thy bread upon the waters: for thou shalt find it after many days. In the morning sow thy seed, and in the evening withhold not thine hand: for thou knowest not whether shall prosper, either this or that, or whether they both shall be alike good."**

Therefore, I would like to point out that as it is with every profession, every relationship, and every family there are persons who behave appropriately and there are those who behave inappropriately. The bible describes this as vessels of honor or dishonor. Furthermore, there is a shocking reality that some people attempt to abuse the financial systems designed to assist the poor and needy. How so you may ask? Well, I am sure if you are at least five years old, you have either seen on TV, read in the newspaper, or have been told by someone about the foster home that had many children who allegedly lived in deplorable conditions even though that family was receiving a substantial amount of money each month for child care.

This type of abuse makes it painfully clear that not all who foster children should do so. Additionally, it also sheds some background on the mind-set of *those* types of foster parents. It appears their mind-set reflects the belief that foster children should be happy to merely have a roof over their heads. That attitude would go on to suggest that the child's emotional needs as well as financial are not important. Sometimes there maybe many levels of abuse and mistreatment to occur in the foster homes. Oftentimes, the abuse/mistreatment is sometimes subtle and not easily recognizable to the child, or other adults.

Now let us look at a situation that may difficult for both foster parent and child. However, I truly believe those foster parents who embrace ministry mindset and are compassionate with their foster child(ren) may not find themselves in this situation. In order for you to under stand this point, I must share some facts with you. State approved foster homes have regulations regarding the number of children and the amount of occupancy space in the home. So for example, if a home is approved for three foster children but one child, Christopher ages out or turns legal age, he may have to leave his foster home. Particularly, if the foster parents desire to foster another child and there is not ample room to meet state requirements. What a blessing it would be if Christopher is able to have his own room. However, in this instance we must consider the size of the family, as well as the home. Furthermore, we must also consider state financial compensation may no longer be available to the foster parents for Christopher's care. Sadly enough, it is at this point Christopher in all probability will not be allowed to remain in his foster home. Please be aware many states have become aware that children in the foster care system will require life skills and ongoing services beyond the young adults eighteenth birthday or legal age. They have incorporated wonderful services to assist foster children prior to and beyond age eighteen (Are you in need of a list of available services? Please check with your local state agency or the web for more details) as the types of services and age limits to continue or qualify to receive these services will once again vary from agency to agency, as well as state to state.

Several years ago, one foster child confided that because he is turning legal age. He is going to have to move out of his foster home. According to the young man, who just turned eighteen, the foster parents told him he will have to move out, as his room is needed for another foster placement, since the state will no longer reimburse them for his care. That young man confided that was his most daunting fear. He went on further to say since he was sixteen years old this was in the back of his mind. He stated, "It is hard but what could I do?" My heart sank to the pit of my stomach and I tried to encourage the young man even though I was holding back my tears. It seemed his eyes asked question "Where is the love?" Let me reiterate, not all foster parents are in child care for monetary purposes. Some foster parents actually love, and recognize the young adults need for continued emotional and financial support throughout their lives.

On the other hand, I will not be biased and leave out that many foster children who are actually blessed to have the opportunity to remain in a foster home placement beyond their eighteenth birthday may choose not to, primarily due to the "Ready to leave home and explore this world on their own syndrome". Additionally, perhaps the young adult embraces the teenage attitude that "I am grown now and I will do as I please." However, for the most part, many foster children who actually wish to remain in their home after their eighteenth birthday may not because the compensation has terminated and the foster family is not willing to house/care for the young adult any longer. For those foster parents who have declared fostering children is "my ministry", but allows that fostering to stop (you know after the reimbursement stops). I cannot help but ask the question, "Was placement an act of ministry or money?" Private and state adoption agencies do a wonderful job of qualifying potential foster parents for financial stability. However, sometimes due to changes in circumstances from month to month, a dependency may develop upon the reimbursement for household maintenance. Therefore, if the foster parent's finances becomes *solely* dependent upon compensation of the foster child's placement in their home, then how can the foster child's needs or the needs of any other child, for that matter be met? Please do not become offended, it is just something to think about! To me, it would not seem that the child's needs or wants (with in boundaries) would be met if there is in fact an on-going financial crisis in the home. Remember I am also referring to private and relative placements as well.

I remember when I was a teenager after my mother died, I had a family from my church, First Evergreen Baptist Church who expressed their interest assisting me during my crucial years of development. However, as it turns out they were really only interested in the three hundred and eighty-seven dollars a month I would receive from my mom and dads death survivor benefits. I know this because I experienced most of the month differential and less than loving treatment. It seemed that my presence was merely tolerated, not appreciated, or celebrated. However, for a few days of the month usually beginning around the thirtieth day of the previous month to about the fifth of the current month, there would always be a sudden interest and care for me. Please note the sudden interests and care did not last long but were only attempts to manipulate me out of my survivor benefits money. What this meant, for those of you who have not figured it out yet is that it appears that people only wanted me in their lives, for monitory reasons. Not only is this theory validated by the way I was treated but also when I declared the bulk of these funds will be saved each month and used for college. Needless to say, I was not in this home very long.

Sometimes, for many children, (like me) in relative or other placements, (non state monitored placements) this can be a common experience. Furthermore, I will not even attempt to elaborate or explain the ordeals some children who have inherited large estates and large sums of money as a result of the death of their parents or guardians. The good thing about this experience for me was that I was at an age where I could make the right decisions for my finances and independent enough to deal with the consequences.

Keep in mind most children are not as ignorant (without knowledge) or naive as they may appear. Children are very cognizant of how they are received and accepted in the family. For example, do you recall this popular bumper sticker? It reads: "Parents be nice to your kids they may have to pick your nursing home!" This suggests to me that adults remember how they were treated as children.

Now back to the lesson at hand. If our society, specifically parents and guardians model family interactions that are motivated by financial gain this teaches a hard lesson in life at an early age about the way they value money more than relationships. You know this type of behavior--let's say "cozying up" which did not begin with me; in fact, **Proverbs 19:6** tells us that **"Many will entreat the favor of the prince: and every man is a friend to him that giveth gifts."** This scripture is great because it is applicable to all relationships, even among friends. It warns that anyone can be subject to valuing money and gifts more than a person or their relationship with that person. So in terms of true friends and finances if you are faced with the challenge of budgeting your finances, regardless of your age, spend your money wisely (save and make investments) as well as choose your friends wisely. In doing so, you will have a better chance to live an emotionally balanced and financially secure life. Do not allow yourself to be deceived, manipulated or caught in the trap of trying to BUY someone's love. Eventually, you will find out in life that true friends are few and far between. You will also find out that real true friends, will celebrate and cherish each other. **Proverbs 18:24** states it like this **"A man that hath friends must shew himself friendly: and there is a friend that sticketh closer than brother."**

Furthermore, giving in terms of time and money will be mutual. Consequently, your needs as well as that of your friend's will be met; and in essence, your giving will not be a one-sided situation. In all honestly, there should be a whole chapter devoted to this topic, but I think for now, you get the picture. If you will ask the Holy Sprit to give you wisdom to manage your inheritance, no matter how big or small and choose your friends, you will be more likely to have wholesome mutually satisfying relationships. Remember Jesus modeled the best characteristics that a friend should have. Furthermore, it behooves everyone to strive to be a friend of Jesus. Let us take a look at **John 15:13-14** as he states, **"Greater love hath no man than this, that a man lay down his life for his friends. Ye are my friends, if ye do whatsoever I command you."**

The final topic in this chapter is directed toward the foster parents, guardians, and all those who endeavor to take on the colossal task of being a foster parent. I think we all can look back and remember moments throughout our lives that were challenging. I am also sure for most of us, we were able to "overcome" those challenging moments because we had the emotional support of someone. That special someone generally offered encouragement and a listening ear during that trial. Perhaps, that someone was the Holy Spirit, or it was Jesus who ministered to your needs through an actual person. The point is no one can make it in this world alone and just as you and I needed the help others to make it in life, so will the children of whom you foster. The emotional and financial support they will need may go beyond age eighteen. So will your foster children have a home in your home for the holidays? Will your foster children still have a welcomed place in your home after they move out at age eighteen if due to uncontrollable circumstances have a need to return home at age thirty? Or if your foster children calls for money will you attempt to help out? What about your biological children? Let us replace the word foster in the phrase foster child and change it to biological. In other words, what would be your attitude if all of the scenarios above were in regard to your biological children? Obviously, there should not be a difference in attitude or assistance for either child, but often there is. Remember we discussed this concern earlier in this chapter. Many foster children are left to fend for themselves as they are asked to leave the only stable home they have ever known, even though they may not be emotionally or financially prepared. After all, I think we all know a family of which there are biological children, who are now adults well beyond age twenty-three; still residing in their parents home and/or their parents are paying for there expenses. Perhaps, maybe even all of them. You may even be one off those parents. If you are there is certainly nothing wrong with that if that is your choice, just keep in mind, just as the biological parent's love and support does not cease at age eighteen, neither should the foster parents' care for the foster child. Now that is something to think about huh? **Isaiah 49 verse 15** poses the question **"Can a woman forget her suckling child, that she should not have compassion on the son of her womb? Yea, they may forget yet will I not forget thee"** However, for those foster parents who are ministry minded and will continue to be a thriving part of the foster child's life even in adulthood, "You are a true blessing and God-send." So I offer thanks to the millions of foster parents through out this world who embrace the "Ministry mindset" and continue to parent their foster children when needed even in their adult years.

My life's journey would not be complete without my acknowledging the earth angels who God sent to minister to my needs when I needed them the most -- beautiful people like Mr. David and Francis Welch. Readers, please be encouraged, as I share this with you. I am sure you know of the home in your neighborhood where all the kids play and congregate. You know, it is where there is always a delicious meal or snack. It's the home where you feel like you're at home, away from home. God blessed the Welches with three biological children. As if their children were not already a handful, they gladly became for me whatever I needed. I appreciate God's favor in my life and the Welches' obedience to God for my sake.

Although the Welches relocated to North Central Louisiana, before my mother died, they still played a vital role in my life. I believe their move was still a part of Gods master plan. After I graduated high school, I attended a Grambling State University, located a few miles in the next town. It just seemed that God was strategically placing people where and when I needed them at different stages in my life. Every thing they have ever done or will do is always appreciated. However, I remember a routine moment that became a very special one and will always hold a special place in my heart. Mrs. Welch and I were shopping at Wal-Mart in

Kim Hood

October 1989. As we leisurely strolled down an isle filled with teddy bears, there was one particular bear that seemed to jump off the shelf and right into my arms. Well, it did not actually jump (smile), I sorta grabbed the bear and put it in the shopping cart (you know where a baby is supposed to ride) Well, I never asked for the bear but the smile and excitement on my face clearly indicated I wanted this bear. Mrs. Welch never said a word to me about the bear. However, she told me to see if her wallet was in the car. When I returned to the store, her purchases were bagged and she was ready to leave. So I told her I did not see the wallet; and she said "Sorry, it was in my pocket!" Will you believe two months went by and December rolled around? To my surprise, Mrs. Welch bought for me the same big teddy bear I pushed around Wal-Mart two months earlier. She gave it to me for Christmas. She then confided that when she sent me to the car for her wallet, she purchased the bear. I named the bear Sunshine because that is what she brought to my life. Even though I am several years older now, I still have Sunshine, the bear, and I still have the Welches. My life has been forever changed for the better simply because of them.

Gloria Meranto is another special lady -- Sis. Gloria, as we call her. She is an anointed woman of God, who pulled no punches and took no prisoners as she ministered to me. This lady taught me every thing she learned and knew about prayer, fasting and holy living.

Right now in America, perhaps, within the last ten years, there has been an emergence of "Christianity". We know that Christianity has been around a while, but the "Cool Christianity" has only recently emerged. We can turn on secular radio stations now and find some Christian music. Additionally, last year cinemas showed movies that were successful in the box office that had a Christian or gospel theme to them.

Sis, Gloria, on the other hand, was a Bible-toting, devil-stomping, without-holiness-you-shall-not-see-God kind of lady; when it was not "cool" or "in" to be so. She is what the world would call fanatical. However, her love, guidance, and walk in the Word of God greatly influences my life. She will never know the impact of her love upon my life. I just thank God for sending this earth angel to me. She is great lady with timeless beauty. Her beauty transcends her outward appearance and seems to encompass her very being. She is truly a Proverbs 31 woman. I remember many days when she would practice her soundtrack in preparation for a solo at church. She would sing many hymns and old 100's around the house. A now favorite of mine is "Bridge Over Troubled Water" she would sang and sang that one song seemingly for hours, and honestly as an unsaved youth it used to bother me to no end (I was into Michael Jackson and Prince, perhaps just as you were). However, she sounded so pretty and it seemed as Jesus himself would sit in the room where she sang. Years later in college I found myself in a lonesome, depressed state. I sobbed uncontrollably as I listened to the radio. I was in an emotionally challenged situation with regard to my severe broken heart. I wondered if things would ever get better. Just as soon as I thought that thought, a miracle happened! For me this was truly a miracle as the radio station (out of the blue) played the song "Bridge Over Troubled Water". I say a miracle, because the station I was tuned in to was not a gospel station but played a mixture of rock and R&B music. When I heard the song I immediately remembered Sis. Gloria singing that song. In my mind I guess I could still hear her, especially as the song played. I then felt my heavy burden lift and had an inner peace that everything is going to be all right. In fact, just as it was years earlier, so it was that day. I felt the presence of God come in my dorm room during that song and my life has not been the same since.

I also remember as a teenager every night before bed, we all read some scriptures from the book of Psalms out loud to each other. Somedays, all I wanted to do was go to sleep and skip the bible readings but this was a daily routine for us and missing the daily Psalms devotion was not an option. I now look back and see how much I treasure the fellowship and value the solid foundation in the word of God that is still beneficial this day.

Did we miss the 4:40 bus to the mall? This is a question I was so grateful to not have to ask any more. For now it was time for my license. I was so anxious to get my drivers license (zoom zoom). Sis Gloria let me borrow her 1986 sporty Buick Skylark (new car back

Kim Hood

then) to practice driving. Can you imagine unleashing an anxious, over zealous, teenager behind the wheel of your new car for driving practice! Well she did so and on many occasions without reservations. In fact, her life was so filled with love for me, she truly embraced me as a part of her family, specifically as her daughter. She treated me just like her daughters she said there is no partiality in this house! She incorporated that philosophy when loving on us, buying things for us, and yes even chastising us (ouch!). Even though today, when we are together we sometimes get a puzzled stare because she is Filipino and I am African American, but she still introduces me as her daughter, still to this day. Even though, we all have our own families and careers we all are very much an intricate part of each others lives. Tesse, AKA Nhing Nhing lives in Oklahoma, Teresa, AKA Mickey lives in Arkansas, Gina, lives in Arkansas, and Debbie, AKA Duck lives in Dallas. I guess it is true what they say a family that prays togethor stays together.

Please do not misunderstand the qualities I have pointed out or the host of wonderful qualities I have failed to mention in each of the angels that I chose to write about. Furthermore, there are other "earth angels" whom I have not mentioned, who have helped me on my journey in life. Their support and encouragement are equally important. However, I do not want to offend anyone as I give God glory for the great things he has done in my life. I know while we are on earth, one of the ways God works is through people. Therefore, people of honor such as Bishop Larry D. Wade and First Lady Debra Wade, of Bethel Temple Community Church in Tyler, Texas, Pastor Robert Barker, Church of God of Prophecy, Alexandria, Louisiana, as well as Prophet Augustine Alacalla from Spain affiliated with the Assemblies of God Church in Ruston, Louisiana, last but certainly not least, Dr. Glenda Carter, then Assistant Vice President of Student Affairs at Grambling State University in Grambling, Louisiana, (A place where everybody is somebody) they have all greatly influenced my life.

The love of God is so rich and vast he reminds us that he is not unrighteous to forget our labor of love that we have shown toward his saints. That is not only good news for those I mentioned but also for those who I could not mention for time's sake (Love Ya! Emma

From a Peasant to a Princess

Dubreil). So please know that if your name has not been written in my book, do not give up! Please keep living for God and perhaps your deeds, as well as your name, will be written in the most important book of all -- The Lamb's Book of Life.

It is better to trust in the lord than to put confidence in man.

Psalm 1 eighteen verse 8

Chapter Four

I Do Not Want To Be Insecure!

When I pose the question, "What character traits are you looking for in a healthy relationship?" The question does not limit the definition of "relationship" to a dating or marriage scenario. It extends beyond the boundaries to cover all our human interactions with one another, from worker to employer, aunt to nephew, and even pet owner to pet (smile!) Let us take a look at some key definitions that will provide further clarity and assistance in understanding the origin of common insecurities that stem from an unstable foundation as a child.

Webster's Dictionary defines secure as to make safe, protect, a state of being safe; confident. To further expound on this, I would like to apply that definition to actual real circumstances. I think it is imperative to the healthy development of a child to have consistent guidance, support, and a solid foundation. To elaborate even further, when a child knows he or she has a place to call home and basic needs are met in that home it creates an environment conducive for proper growth and nurturing. On the other hand, if these elements are missing from the child's life, often that child is forced to grow up quickly by assuming roles he or she is not mentally mature to handle. For example, the home where the father figure is not present and the mother for what ever reason resorts to discussing the financial concerns of the home with her eight year old. Or we may also look at the family that has a large sibling group but the parents are not able to provide enough food and adequate clothing for all. This may force the eldest child to obtain employment in their school years to contribute the basic necessities of the family. Now please do not misunderstand that last example as I think it is healthy for teens to learn and grow into adulthood as they become more aware of the adult responsibilities they will some day have. (A J-O-B) However, there is an added element of adult stress on a teenager who works merely to give all of their check to mom or dad, on a consistent basis, to pay bills that the parents would normally cover. The operative word in this scenario is ALL.

Typically, teens in a more financially stable home environment may contribute a portion of their earned money as a learning tool for responsibility, not out of obligation. Furthermore, they can reap the rewards of their labor by deciding what to do with their money. Some financial flexibility may be the incentive to encourage the teen to grasp a good work ethic through out their life.

When I was in college, we studied several theories that expound more in depth on the "needs" of a human being. Let us look at Abraham Maslow's theory as he stated "A hierarchy of human needs based on two groupings: deficiency needs and growth needs." "Within the deficiency needs, each lower need must be met before moving the next higher level." He further elaborated that "If at some future time, a deficiency is detected, the individual will act to remove the deficiency." According to Maslow, "an individual is ready to change or grow if and only if the deficiency needs are met." Abraham Maslow categorized his theory in terms of a pyramid or hierarchy to specifically address the order of which needs should be met. Level one is physiological needs: hunger thirst, bodily comforts etc.; level two is safety/security: out of danger; level three is belonging and love: affiliate with others, be accepted; level four is esteem: to achieve, be competent, gain approval and recognition, level five is cognitive: to know, to understand, and explore; level six is Aesthetic: symmetry, order and beauty; level seven is self-actualization: to find self fulfillment and realize one's potential; and finally level eight is self-transcendence: to connect to something beyond the ego or to help others find self-fulfillment and realize their potential. All of these levels are pretty much self explanatory.

With all that said, let us talk about the millions of children who do not have their basic needs met throughout the world. Furthermore, let us ponder a moment about the thousands of children in the United States who are not accepted by their families; which also includes subsequent placements such as some private relative, foster, and adoptive homes. Consequently, the children may never get the encouragement, recognition, and love they need to develop a healthy sense of self worth. These may be the children who "act out" and have horrible behavioral problems. Sometimes, the behavioral problems range from theft, manipulation, gross exaggerations, lying, food hoarding (often done because the child is not accustomed to having food on a regular basis), so that child may horde food because of the fear that their food supply will be cut off, night mares, sleep walking, bed wetting, animal abuse, defying authority, sexual dysfunction's in adult years, as well as inappropriate sexual ideation's or sexual encounters as a child or teenager. Fighting other siblings at home or at school or bullying may also become a part of the child's undesired behavior, as well. I say undesired behavior because I do not believe the child who acts out, initially does so on an intentional basis. No one wants to feel insecure and as a result exhibit inappropriate and intolerable behaviors. However, it is when the child attempts to find their place in the home and be loved for who they are flaws and all, many times the child is not accepted into the family because of the behaviors. You see often times when biological parents produce a child, they have the opportunity to grow and love together, establish a bond if you will. The majority of the time, when the biological child exhibits inappropriate behaviors, most parents are willing to endure the behavior, and dismiss the behavior by saying they will grow out of it. However, when a foster child is placed in a home and begins to act out often times some foster parents are not willing to be patient with the child or endure the behavior(s). This happens typically in the adjustment phase; which ironically occurs after the "Honeymoon phase". It is in this phase the child begins to relax and test boundaries. It would be great if the foster parent would incorporate this into their home during this stage, as lasting relationship is under construction. Now please note, in this scenario, it is assumed that the child placed in the foster home and the foster parents are on qualified levels for supervision, i.e., a level three child is placed in a home of which the foster parents have been through training and can effectively supervise a child who is a level three or above. The unfortunate side of the same scenario is sometimes a level three child may actually exhibit behaviors of a level four or five child, and due to the safety of the child and others, the child will require a more restrictive environment. If you are a foster parent and have been in this or similar situations, I am not referring to you. My intent is to provide a unique perspective and perhaps understanding of the child's needs for stability and love, when the safety of the child and your family is *not* in question.

Therefore, if the foster parents lobby for a different placement for the child and/ or are emotionally unavailable to the child, this will reinforce the reality of the child's insecurities. So then, I think the average reader, regardless of their upbringing, can understand at least on a minimal level that the struggle some orphans and foster children go through in an effort to fit in "the norm" and "earn the approval" of their foster parents and siblings can be quite challenging to say the least. Most children who have found themselves in this position will agree that insecurities often develop because they feel they have to work to fit in, and this obviously is a long process. However, they may find that they never really truly fit in. As with anything, there are some exceptions to the rules. So I thank God for those many exceptions with regard to successful foster home placements. However, for the purpose of this book, I am addressing the percentage of the population who have not been apart of the successful placements.

Some foster children reported sometimes they feel like they have to compete with other children in the home - natural or adoptive - for the attention, love and acceptance of the parents. Sadly enough, the emotional needs of the foster child may have been neglected so long from past or perhaps a current placement, that insecurities have taken hold of that child. The other side to this emotional rollercoaster may be that the foster parents and new sibling group are reaching out in love but the foster child is not in an emotional state to receive their love now, patience will be the key. The child may now embrace a mindset that "I do not deserve to be loved or I am not good enough". However, the truth is simply because you (the child) were not treated correctly; with love, respect, and your needs provided for, does not mean that you are not a worthy individual. What it does mean is that you will have to forgive your natural parents and foster parents /or those who were supposed to meet your needs and did not. (See the next chapter on Anger!) Please note that you do not have to be insecure. I give you permission to let go of your insecurities and trust God to heal and provide for all of your needs through those he has placed in your life to be a blessing to you. Please also know, this means that you will have to read, study and allow God through the Holy Spirit to transform and reveal to you who you are in Christ Jesus, and by doing so, you can break the cycle of abuse in your life.

In fact the word of God declares in the book of **Ephesians chapter 1 verse 5 and 6 "that having predestined unto us unto the adoption of children by Jesus Christ to himself, according to the good pleasure of his will. To the praise of the glory of his grace, wherein he hath made us accepted in the beloved."** So then you see you may not have earthly parents to meet your needs. However, if you will allow Jesus to provide for your needs, you may find that his care exceeds the care of your earthly parents. He may do this by placing others in your life to help care and be a positive influence for you. Jesus's love is so vast and his ways are so astounding no one can predict how he may choose to work on your behalf. Your goal then is to simply be a willing vessel. Remember **Psalms 27 verse 10** states, **"When my father and mother forsook me, then the Lord will take me up."** Is not that the best of the best news? For we know that you are never alone in this great big old world, even if it feels like we are sometimes. Please also keep in mind that our emotions and feelings are sometimes fleeting and can be unstable at times. Therefore, our emotions should never be the basis of which we use to determine our heavenly father's love toward us. His love and care for us is constant and I have found that he often love and care for us, even when we do not care or love our selves. So for that I give our loving heavenly father three cheers and shout "Thanks be unto our God who gives us the victory through Christ Jesus!"

Make no friendship with an angry man; and with a furious man thou shalt not go.
Lest thou learn his ways, and get a snare to thy soul.

Proverbs Chapter 22 verses 24 & 25

Chapter Five

Anger!

Now it is time for us to entertain this nasty little emotion (Smile). Wow, what a negative way to describe anger. Actually, anger is a natural emotion. It is often how we choose to express ourselves when angry that makes our perception of anger positive or negative. The truth about anger is that it is a God given emotion that should be used to fuel positive changes in our lives. However, most people were not taught to express themselves appropriately when angry. Anger then becomes a handicap instead of an enhancement. In the Book of **Ephesians, Chapter 4, part of verse 26 plainly** states **"Be ye angry, and sin not."** This is the perfect scriptural reference for us to know how God feel about anger and the way Christians should respond when angry.

Anger is often the vehicle many foster children use to express their fears, hurts, resentments, and down right disgust for the path in life they are on. Many times abused, foster, and adoptive children have been in multiple placements with other children who are in the same situation as they are...that is to say they are without appropriate guidance, nurture and support from a parent, on a consistent basis. Consequently, the vehicles of expressions learned often times, are not the most appropriate or acceptable. **Proverbs chapter 16 verse 32 tells us "he that is slow to anger is better than the mighty; and he that ruleth his spirit than he that taketh a city."** In an effort to express anger appropriately, we have to correctly identify the source of our anger. Please note each person will have their own unique source or sources of anger.

Well, why do I need to identify my emotions you might ask? The answer is simply because it is the first step to your emotional healing. You see you have to know what your issues are before you can confront them. It's like a visit to your doctor, the doctor cannot simply prescribe a general medication to stop your pain; without first evaluating you, thereby allowing you the opportunity to tell her what is bothering you. After the doctor has correctly identified what your concern is, a prescription will be issued for that specific ailment.

It is also important to identify your emotions as a child (or even as an adult, as it is never too late). By doing so, you will not allow other negative forms of inappropriate behaviors such as jealousy, control, bitterness, and wrath to remain a part of your character.

As humans, we all experience at some point or time the so called negative emotions. However, there is a big difference in one's ability to have a negative emotion, process through it then release it, that's being free. Please see **I John chapter 1 verse 9** as it states **"If we confess our sins, he is faithful and just enough to forgive us our sins, and to cleanse us of all unrighteousness."** On the other hand to hold on to a negative emotion(s) and allow them to become a part of your personal being is not only detrimental to your health but to your emotions as well.

I am not an expert on the psychosis of anger, however, let me see if I can from personal experience apply an example to situations more commonly experienced among foster children. Let us address the child who has been deprived of the positive attention from their parents. As a live-in counselor in several group homes, I have found some emotionally disturbed children and teens, who did not receive parental attention and support (either from a natural parent or parent type figure), had a tendency to act out. By acting out, the child almost always gets the attention he or she desires, even though it is in a negative manner.

So initially, I was tempted to think the children were simply terrible little monsters with anger issues. When I embraced the ministry mindset it was easier for me to minister to the needs of the children that the Lord placed in my life for that season. For you see,

I had to be comforted in my childhood in the same manner. By age fifteen, I was an orphan and I began to deal with all the emotions, embarrassment, and despair of losing both parents at an early age. Jesus reminds us that we should comfort those by the same measure where with we ourselves were comforted.

So as a live-in counselor, I was able to resist the temptation to take the children's negative behavior personally. I understood that in this case anger was not the issue, but perhaps was this child's way of asking for some more attention. At this point, it was clear that child had not learned to identify his feelings and ask for what he needed.

In all honesty, I would not be wrong if I stated there are many adults who have not yet learned to identify their feelings, process, and appropriately express their emotions. This is one of the ways the cycle of anger is passed down from generation to generation. However, you can make a difference in your life and that of your children by breaking the cycle. How do I do that you ask? Well, you can break the cycle of anger by allowing the Holy Spirit to teach and deliver you from anger. In the mean time, you can be open to learn better, more productive ways to live your life, starting at the age you are now. Furthermore, determine in your heart that you will learn, study, and be open to wise Godly counsel. Please note your counsel should come primarily from the bible. Every solution to every problem is found in the word of God. You will also find that a wealth of wisdom that can be found in other people of whom the Lord will place in your life. Be humble enough to receive guidance from people such as your pastor, teachers, counselors, or youth minister. If God placed them in your life, it is for a reason. In conjunction with the instruction of the Holy Spirit and the bible they will provide the support you need to overcome anger. Please also utilize the wealth of knowledge that is found on this and related topics, perhaps located in self-help sections of your local bookstore, Library or even on line. The point is, be open to what the Lord has in store for you and be willing to do it.

To appoint unto them that mourn in Zion, to give unto them beauty for ashes, the oil of joy for mourning, the garment of praise for the spirit of heaviness; that they might be called trees of righteous, the planting of the lord, that he might be glorified.

Isaiah chapter 61 verse 3

Chapter Six

Fourteen Going on Twenty-Four!

This will probably be the most difficult, yet most needed chapter. I say that because the topic of sex is always a touchy subject. However, as the name of the chapter would suggest; many of our children grow-up too fast. Thanks to TV, the Internet, uncensored music, as well as the lack of parental guidance, our children could be destined to be improperly influenced. Consequently, some children are left to embrace as truth standards of living that are immoral and corrupt. Additionally, the generation curse or cycle of incest, child molestation, and sexual inappropriateness has contributed to the dementia and moral demise in families.

It would be a gross misrepresentation on my part, to not point out what has already been established by the Bible. It is a sin to engage in sexual activity outside of the institution of marriage. There are so many dynamics that I could discuss regarding this matter. However, please note that this book has been birth through the struggles and victories I have experienced. My experiences good and bad; help to develop my character and Christ-like qualities I possess today through the power of the Holy Spirit. Therefore, Christ and his principles are the basis for my success and this topic as well. So as I continue to define appropriate relationships according to biblical standards, let us see how the bible defines marriage. **Genesis chapter 2 verse eighteen** says **"And the Lord God said, "It is not good that the man should be alone: I will make him an help meet for him. Therefore shall a man leave his father and his mother, and shall cleave unto his wife:**

and they shall be one flesh" Moreover, **Hebrews chapter 13 verse 4** tells us **"Marriage is honorable in all, and the bed undefiled: but whoremongers and adulteress God will judge."** Furthermore, you may ask why are these definitions are necessary?

Well, these definitions are necessary to understand what is appropriate and holy, according to the guidelines established by our heavenly father regarding sexual intimacy. So then I can clearly state again any type of sexual activity outside the institution of marriage is sin.

Now let us apply everything that we have read to circumstances that sometimes occur in some foster/adoptive homes, some residential treatment/group home centers, and even in some private homes. There are many foster/adoptive children who have been sexually abused by their natural parent(s), or relative(s), or strangers at one point in their lives. Pleases note that not only is this a sin but it is a crime. So once again, if you are reading this book and are being abused in any manner, please report it to an adult you can trust and the proper authorities.

Additionally, many of the same children continue to experience sexual abuse by the hand of other older children in subsequent placements but particularly in group and foster homes, as they a channeled through the system. The sexual abuse is not only limited to other teens "acting out" on other children. Even more sad, there are some foster placements that are not suitable or appropriate because of the sexual abuse perpetrated by a foster parent or relative in their placement. Please understand children often mimic what they see adults do whether it is good or bad. Traditionally, a child develops their sense of self worth based upon the way they are treated by the adults in their lives. So then, you can easily see how detrimental sexual abuse is to children as they are subject to the unwanted degradation of inappropriate touching, fondling, and molestation. Please note sexual abuse does not discriminate. There are just as many boys who are sexually abused as there are girls, for these boys, their ordeal may be even more difficult to heal. For we know in general boys are socialized and passionately encouraged to be strong, not cry, or express feelings. Therefore, any attempts by the male child to ask for help, may be perceived by that child as weak and not man like behavior.

In actuality, that perception could not be further from the truth. We have the primary responsibility to care for ourselves and love ourselves. Asking for help, when we are not being treated right is a part of that care and responsibility we have to our selves. In other words, it is having a healthy since of self-esteem. (See chapter 3 on insecurities) To put it simply, if you do not care about yourself, then who will?

That question, as cold and hard as it seems, appears to bring about another point. That point is to the pure in heart, one would think that adults who parent would know better than to abuse or mistreat children, but that is often not the case. So what do you say to the innocent, beautiful, and developing fourteen year old girl, who suddenly experiences unwanted glares, a sudden invasion of privacy, as well as sexual inappropriateness that includes comments and touching by her step-father? or What do you say to the adolescent boy who is pressured to fit in with his peers at the group home and is told "You have to sexually act out" in order to be accepted or even protected from others? These are simply horrible and deplorable circumstances many children have to overcome, in addition to the normal adolescent challenges, simply to survive. Consequently, in an attempt to provide the best and least restrictive placement for the child(ren), they are moved from home to home, shelter to shelter and/or residential treatment center to residential treatment center. This type of instability only seems to compound the emotional unrest and despair of the child. Keep in mind that even though the child may be delivered from the immediate threat of sexual abuse by changing surroundings, the trauma from the abuse has oftentimes become a part of the child. Therefore, if the child comes from a home where manipulation was the essential way to get needs met, then that child is taught to manipulate.

It is now, therefore, very imperative for adults who foster children to attend training's, educate themselves, and be open to what we deem as typical behaviors exhibited by abused and neglected children. Our foster brother and sisters are a special needs group that may require more understanding, more compassion, and more grace than the needs of your biological children.

Well, how can you say that? You may ask? I can say that because the temptation is always present to give up on foster children when they "act out", simply because they are *not* biological children. For further clarification, keep reading as everything will soon tie together.

Meanwhile, a unique aspect about this book is that it offers encouragement for both the orphans/foster child, and for the foster parent, as well. This is great news because the Lord's grace and healing powers are not limited to a certain set of people. Consequently, through the anointing of the Holy Spirit everyone can receive healing and restoration. In addition to your emotions and inner man being restored through the irrevocable works of the Holy Spirit, I want to suggest to you practical concepts.

To state it plainly you may have been subject to abuses and maltreatment, however, that is not your fault. Please note during that period in your life, you were a victim. However, this is a new day for you, a new beginning. Your new beginning should start with a new mindset by throwing away the "victim mentality" and embracing the "victor mindset". Well, you may ask what is the difference? Let's take a look. A victim is a person who suffers abuse, hurt, or any type of personal loses by the acts of another person. A victim mentality is a mind set that says I am dependent upon others to succeed or change. Somehow, the victim mentality allows a person to remain vulnerable to abuse, misuse, and maltreatment. A victor is someone who may experience setbacks, disappointments, and challenges *but* overcomes them. It does not matter how difficult things may seem, a victor never gives up, never! A victor chooses to win! Therefore, it may be true you have every reason to have a bitter attitude and be sour about the events that took place in your life. However, you must ask yourself will a negative, bitter attitude change the past? The answer is no! A negative bitter attitude, will only make you a less desirable person to interact with. Most assuredly many of the people of whom you encounter today are not the people who have inflicted harm upon you. Therefore, for them it will be difficult to understand your misguided emotions. Perhaps, you have treated them like they owe you something, by interacting with them in anger, or indifference.

On the other hand if you embrace the victor mindset, you will begin to set in motion your healing. **Romans chapter 8 verse 28 which states "And we know that all things work together for good to them that love God, to them who are called according to his purpose."** You will also find that a victor mind set does not deny or minimize the abuse/neglect you have experienced but it empowers you survive in spite of the abuse. As you learn more about your purpose in Christ, you will begin to grow step by step. The practical application of that is you will move from surviving abuse to becoming more than a conqueror in every area of your life. When this occurs you will know how to make healthy, God inspired choices for your life, in terms of your relationships and behaviors regarding your sexuality. You will see yourself the way God, your father sees you. Once you realize your heavenly father's love for you, through your power of choice, you will demand that others value and treat you that way that you deserve to be treated, as well.

In Two Thousand and Three, the number of children adopted into families decreased by three point eight percent with only fifty thousand children adopted according the US Department of Health and Human Services.

Chapter Seven

A Home for the Holidays?

This is a common phrase used among college students and our brave brothers and sisters, who serve in the armed forces. Some may ponder where to spend the holidays during their next period of leave, as opportunities for travel and foreign studies present themselves. However, as refreshing and heart felt as these words are, "Going home for the holidays!" For many people, that phrase can be both heart wrenching and dreadful. "Others" may include many hurting individuals even though they are a thriving part of a family unit. However, for the purposes of this book we will address the population of children, teens, and adults who do not have a family to call their own to help celebrate special occasions such as birthdays and holidays. These are all notable occasions, but without mom, dad, or the person(s) we have come to know as mom and dad present to share proud moments, they can seem really sad. Ironically enough, that statement is true for orphans of all ages. Typically when we think of orphans we think of children; however, if it is God's will, orphaned children grow up to be adults and consequently deal with childhood issues along the line of abandonment and self esteem in their adult years.

    Therefore, the pain is just as real for those persons who are not blessed to have their parents and guardians in their adult years. The bottom line poses a question; how do we handle those special moments? How do we get over the fact that my biggest fan or cheerleader, otherwise known as "mom" for some. Perhaps, it was "dad" for others, is not here to share my life? Well, let's review a few Biblical facts that may offer further explanations regarding the system the Lord has established regarding life. If nothing else, this scripture will provide a reminder that we will all keep our final appointment with eternity sooner or later. In the meantime, **Ecclesiastics** reminds us in **chapter 3 verse 1** that **"to every thing there is a season, and a time to every purpose under the heaven:"** Therefore, we understand that the earth in its entirety are on the system of seed time and harvest. Simply put we will experience various seasons in our lives. However before we experience a time of harvest, we must go through the planting and watering seasons.

When some Christians speak of harvest time, often they are referring to financial principles. However, the seed time and harvest principle is quite relevant in other areas of our lives. Seasons include good, bad, happy, and yes, even sad events that often come to help us developed Godly characteristics. To look at this further, we also know that in any given season, we have the opportunity to sow good or productive seeds during the sow season. This will ensure that the good seeds we have sown will produce a good harvest. Please be aware just as it is in the case of the good or productive seed; it is also applicable to the bad or unproductive seeds we sow. For we know that seeds in general represent a beginning, the development, or new life if you will of the type of seed planted. Perhaps, it is an orange, perhaps it is a tree, or perhaps, it may even be a beautiful little baby.

The Book of Psalms also tells us that our life is but a vapor. Therefore, we should value the time, no matter how long or short, we are granted with our parents and/or guardians. We can also note that some of us did not have as much time to spend with our parents. However, we are still blessed. I think it's important that we take comfort in the fact that we all can strive to cherish and remember our parents and guardians. In doing so, we keep a part of them alive. Special moments like mom conning you into going to the doctor: You'll find that she gently held your hand as you received your shot, then took you out for ice cream afterwards. Or perhaps the dad who let you work on the model car, or the real one

From a Peasant to a Princess

in the garage. You were right there as dad wiped grease off his hand and asked for a wrench. As you handed him the correct tool and his face lights up and he replies that's my boy! Oh yes! We cannot forget a visit to grandmother or mydea's who always had a delicious pound cake or chocolate cake on the table that simply melted in your mouth. How special it was when you showed her your report card filled with A's, she smiled and gave you her credit card, then retorted go get whatever you want and keep up the good work! Each and every one of us has our own special moments with mom, dad or guardians.

It is your responsibility to keep their legacy alive in your life. In doing so, you allow yourself to honor, process, and acknowledge that relationship even though that person is no longer here.

Check out this list of creative ideas to remember your loved ones:

1. Listen to their favorite song or a song that reminds you of the special time you shared.
2. Read an old letter they wrote to you.
3. Read their favorite Bible scripture.
4. In the game of charades, respectfully imitate them.
5. Cook their favorite meal.
6. Write a letter to them and update them on all the things that have happened in your life, since they have gone on to be with the Lord.

[Let me interject a needed scripture here. **I Corinthians chapter 4 verse 14** says: **"For if we believe that Jesus died and rose again, even so them also which sleep in Jesus will God bring with him."** In this scripture, he is referring to the second coming of Christ. So you see, not only does Christ offer us power to strive to live sin free in this world, but he also provides salvation and comfort when we die or sleep in Christ.] Now let us get back to the list. You may want to:

7. Name your first-born (or next) child after them.
8. Keep their favorite Christmas ornament(s) as a part of your Christmas traditions.
9. Buy your loved one's favorite perfume or cologne and take a whiff of it every now and then.
10. Finally, let us not forget that a picture is worth a thousand words.

The list can go on and on; but whatever items or events you determine are special, use them to keep your memories alive.

Now let us talk about "the most wonderful time of the year." You know -- the season where jingle bells began to ring, stockings are hung by chimney with care as the sweet smell of warm cinnamon fills the air. If you guessed the Christmas season, you guessed right. We celebrate the birth of our savior Jesus Christ (the only true meaning of Christmas).

This is supposed to be a fun and happy time of year; but for many it is not. I would be limited in my thinking to suggest that orphans and foster children are the only ones who may have a difficult time emotionally this time of year. The truth is this may be a concern for others as well.

However, I am writing this book from an orphan's perspective -- distinctly from my personal experiences as an orphan and from having worked with children as well as adults who are orphans.

Please note, down through the years, the Holy Spirit through fellowship with him has taught me to overcome feelings of depression, anger, and loneliness, especially during the holidays and birthdays. In addition to the awesome fellowship I have with him, I enjoy the remaining family members and friends in my life. Secondly, the Holy Spirit taught me to create the holiday season that I want. You see my friend, oftentimes, some people fall into the trap of waiting for someone else to provide for their needs whether emotional or physical. They may not realize that they have the power through the Holy Spirit to meet some of their own needs.

Ironically, we can do that through meeting the need of others. I have discovered on my journey in life that it did not matter how tough situations became for me; there was always someone in a worst predicament. Always! Therefore, I learned to count my blessings, thank God that things are as well as they are, and praise Him because he is going to make things better. Just in case you did not know, we serve an **Ephesians chapter 3 and verse 20 God who is able to do exceedingly and abundantly above all that we ask or think, according to the power that worketh in us!** So as you experiment ways to remember your special loved one, be sure to incorporate these practical emotional wellness tips. These tips may be things you are already doing. If not, then try at least three activities from the list above find out how instrumental they are in your healing process.

Here are a few points to consider as you effectively go through your healing process:

1. Keep in mind it is normal to miss loved ones who are no longer living. (Sleeping)
2. Keep in mind that age, depth of the relationship, and number of years your loved one has gone on to be with the Lord, are all factors to consider. Grief and anger are sometimes experienced because after we honor them, we desire to be with them again but cannot. Therefore we may feel anger and helplessness because there is absolutely nothing we can do to bring our deceased loved one(s) back. Furthermore, the duration of the grieving process varies with each individual.
3. Allow the Holy Spirit to comfort you he will put things into perspective for you. His love is filled with such understanding and compassion that one hug or one touch from him will heal all pain. You will begin to understand the deeper meaning and higher purpose of your destiny and even of those who have gone on. It is then when you can grasp the concept that we are all just pilgrims journeying through this pilgrim land and this place is not our home. We can then realize that some good-byes are not forever.

He raiseth up the poor out of the dust, And lifteth up the beggar from the dunghill, to set them among princes, and to make them inherit the throne of glory: for the pillars of the earth are the Lord's and he hath set the world upon them.

First Samuel Chapter Two verse eight.

Chapter Eight

You Can Make It!

From a Peasant to a Princess: what an eye-catching title for this book! I bet there were many people who thought this was a typical book about fairy tale knights and dragons. Perhaps, others thought it was one of many twists to the well-known Cinderella story. In essence, it may be a combination of all.

I lived my life, as most people do as peasant. I gladly accepted living underneath the privileges my heavenly father had for me. I did that simply because I did not know there was a better way for me. In my early years I allowed the negative vicissitudes of life to get the best of me. How did you do that you may ask? The peasant mindset became a dominant factor in my life. I often defined myself by the trials I went through. I also quite often found myself comparing myself and my accomplishments (or lack thereof) to that of other people, particularly peers who had parents. I often wondered how much further could I be in life, if I had as much support as Becky or Sherri! I often thought about the types of emotional pitfalls I could have avoided if I simply had my dad around to shelter and guide me. As a young person I seemed to experience more than my fair share of trials, which often seemed insurmountable at times. The trials I faced proved to be very taxing on my sprit to say the least. During this season in my life, I thought I did not have any hope or evidence that my life would get any better. I had a little faith (or so I thought) but the faith I had would almost always be misdirected, because I put my faith in people, in opportunities, and in my endeavors. Sadly I did so without putting my faith in God first. Of course, at the time I was a teenager and went to church faithfully most weeks. Primarily, I went out of tradition and to satisfy my moral ego, just as millions of people do today. You may even be one of those persons. If so, there is hope for you just as it was for me! My moral ego, as I call it, suggested that if I attend church and comply with a couple of the Ten Commandments: that I have completed all the requirements necessary to go to heaven upon my death. The fallacy with that thinking, is that Jesus is so much more than a Wednesday or Sunday experience. He is real and desires to be an intricate part of every area in our lives. He challenges us to learn of him and discover the deep hidden things of his kingdom. The deep hidden things he is in reference to can only be obtained through a personal relationship with him. It was not until I met Jesus Christ, that I began to feel hope. I begin to think that just as things suddenly went wrong for me, they can suddenly turn for my good. So in my meeting with Jesus, he brought joy, he brought the strength and victory I so desperately needed in my life.

Jesus provided the encouragement I needed to believe him for the victory in adversarial situations even though, many circumstances seemed negative. It was through his love, he began a wonderful transformation on my inner man. The transformation was so awesome and astounding that my life has not been the same since. My whole perspective has changed and I no longer entertain a victim mentality. I can gladly embrace the unconditional love of my heavenly father and know there is nothing that can separate me again from his love! Wow, it feels so good to know that I am loved unconditionally. You see in Christ, you do not have to earn his love or perform works to measure up as an attempt to gain his love. He simply loves you because you are you! **Ephesians chapter 1 verses 5 and 6** explains it like this: **Having predestined us unto the adoption of children by Jesus Christ to himself, according to the good pleasure of his will. To the praise of the glory of his grace wherein he hath made us accepted into the beloved.** What is even more astounding is that he loves you enough to not leave you the same.

From a Peasant to a Princess

Is not that simply wonderful to know? Know what you ask? Know that you are loved and accepted by your heavenly father. As you grow and become spiritually mature, you will get a revelation that the above statement is a very powerful and liberating. You will be able to face your critics and those who have rejected you with the love and understanding of our heavenly father. Furthermore, as you embrace your love and acceptance in Christ Jesus you will be able to embrace a healthy sense of self-worth that God intended for you to have. You will now be able to take confidence my friend, as you are a part of a well devised plan that originated before you were born. You are not an accident! Please know that God knew you before you were born and has great things in store for you. **Jeremiah chapter 29 verse 11** states, **"For I know the thoughts that I think toward you, saith the Lord, thoughts of peace, and not of evil, to give you an expected end."** It is also wonderful to know that God further proved his love by sending his son Jesus to provide us an opportunity to be a part of the Kingdom of God. **John chapter 3 verse 16** declares **"For God so loved the world, that he gave his only begotten son, that whosoever will shall not perish, but have everlasting life."** Furthermore, Jesus laid down his life for us. He loved us so much that he was willing to die as a living sacrifice for our sins. Did you know that if you were the only person in the world, Jesus would still have died for you? Simply put, when he was on the cross you were in his heart and on his mind.

So you can see it was only when I received this revelation knowledge that I was able to embrace who I really am through Christ Jesus. I am able to embrace my inheritance through Christ in the Kingdom of God. I believe **I Peter Chapter 2 verse 9** sums it up eloquently as it clearly states **"But ye are a chosen generation, a royal priesthood, an holy nation, a peculiar people; that ye should show forth the praises of him who hath called you out of darkness into his marvelous light."** Therefore, from one Princess to another Princess (or Prince) you can make it on your journey in life. You can make the Godly choices needed in order to live a prosperous, holy life. God has equipped you with every thing you will need for your journey. You must simply explore those gifts and talents and use them for the benefit of the Kingdom of God.

Through God you can forgive those who have hurt you. You can go on to live a whole emotionally sound life. Please note, every one has challenges in life but it's up to you to choose to overcome them through Christ. The important thing is to never give up, do not ever give up! Do not give up on yourself and certainly, do not give up on God!

If you get some bulldog faith in God and dare to believe him to bring every promise he has for you to pass in this lifetime, you will soon come to realize that with God on your side, you cannot fail as **Romans chapter 8 verses 31** reminds us **"What shall we then say to these things? If God be for us, who can be against us?"** So believe in your yourself, believe in your dreams and believe in your God (God of Abraham, Isaac, and Jacob, you know Jesus's father.) Then you will soon discover with God the impossible, becomes possible. My friend, embrace those thoughts as you face your challenges and choose to overcome them.

Did you know through the blood of Jesus, you will experience victory and soon find that your royal journey has not stopped at simply becoming a Princess or a Prince (Chief, ruler, magistrate, one having authority) in the Kingdom of God but one day, according to scripture you (we) will actually rule with him. Let us look at **II Timothy chapter 2 verse 12** as it says **"If we suffer, we shall also reign with him: if we deny him, He also will deny us:"**, to me that is exciting news. It's exciting to know simply because, it all goes back to our beginning, when we were created to rule and have dominion in this earthly realm. Let me point out even today in this earth realm some countries are still governed by Kings and dictatorships. Many Kings and Queens who currently reign or who are next in line for the throne have what we call "Royal Blood". That means their birth lineage pass on from one generation to next and they inherit their position as sole dictator of their country with the title King or Queen. Ironically, the same is true as well for children of the most high God. God made us royalty when we were born and it is up to us to decide if we will take our rightful place in the Kingdom of God, as children who rule and operate in the power and authority over what God has committed into our hands (earthly inheritance).

From a Peasant to a Princess

A major part of our wonderful inheritance, include spiritual authority. Spiritual authority is needed when you face obstacles and opposition when trying to complete an assignment from our heavenly father. Your first step to receiving your inheritance involves salvation by inviting Christ to be the Lord of every area of your life. Please allow the Holy Spirit to touch the inner depths of your heart as we pray, please repeat out loud:

Dear Heavenly father, I come to you in your son Jesus' name. I thank you for hearing my prayers and for seeing all the tough times that I have come through. I thank you for being with me in those times, even if it felt like I was all alone. My life up until this point has not been the best, so I ask you to take my life and make it what you will. I repent of all my sins! I denounce all evil and I give you Lord Jesus, permission to heal my every hurt and forgive my every sin. So I boldly confess Jesus Christ as my Lord and Savior and I believe in my heart that God raised Jesus from the dead. Now I ask the Holy Spirit to sanctify me and dwell in my heart forever!!!

Welcome to our royal family, my brother or my sister in Christ. Now you are on your way! It is very important for you to read and study the instruction manual your heavenly father left you, in order to effectively rule your domain. Manual? What are you talking about big sister Kim? What are you referring to? Well, I am glad you asked! The Bible is the manual that I am referring to! It contains the very heart of our Father. He provides guidance and counsel for us through his living word. He offers clear instructions on how to enjoy successful holy living on earth and how to obtain a great eternal retirement plan, as well (Smile). If you read the word of God, apply the word of God; and bind it upon your heart, you will find it to be like a sweet healing ointment, that you can rub on to soothe the scraps, cuts, and bruises (metaphorically speaking) that your spirit man will experience.

Take note, it is now time for you to be rooted and grounded in a local church body, if you currently are not. Our heavenly Father has designed the Pastor and the church body in which he plants us (or will place you soon) as your support system. You will need the fellowship of other born-again believers to assist you on you journey in life. Meanwhile, the bible tells us that the Angels rejoice over one sinner that comes unto Christ. So if you prayed that prayer from your heart and you are truly repentative-let us celebrate with them as heaven is hosting a party right now as we speak in your honor!

Now, if you have previously taken the first step to accept your rightful place in the Kingdom of God by receiving Christ's salvation, my prayer for you is that you will continue to allow the precious Holy Spirit to teach and guide your every decision as you grow in Christ, from faith to faith and glory to glory. Henceforth, my prayer is that you continue to discover who you are in Christ and what you are called to do for the Kingdom of God. **Matthew chapter 10 verse one and eight** offers this **"And when he called unto Him His twelve disciples, He gave them power against unclean spirits, to cast them out, and to heal all manner of sickness and all manner of disease. Heal the sick, cleanse the lepers, raise the dead, cast out devils: freely ye have received, freely give"** Many people may think this mandate is limited to the disciples and is no longer applicable to born again believers of this day. However, let me suggest that God is the same yesterday, today, and forevermore. Take confidence in the general mission of the Kingdom of God that "soul winning" (fishers of men) and living an abundant life will never fade away. You will find as you continue your walk with God, the tasks he has specifically assigned for your hands to do. I hope you will execute the plan of God for your life through the grace, love, power and authority of Jesus Christ. Amen.

"And the Lord shall deliver me from every evil work, and will preserve me unto His heavenly kingdom: to Whom be glory for ever and ever. Amen."

II Timothy chapter 4 verse 18

EL Corizon de la Princesa
(The Heart of the Princess)

I often wonder if the pain will ever pass. Some days were so horrible, the hurt I can no longer mask.

Twenty-two years gone but it still feels like yesterday, that sad moment when Betty went away. Her love was so deep it will never fade as I keep it fresh, by loving others in that very same way!

My heavenly father said I am here my child to supply your need. I will never leave nor forsake you my dear my love for you will always be here!

Through the storm and through the fire your separation from her is but for little while…For you see just as I love you I also love Betty too!

The day will come when we will all be as one. Then my Glory shall be revealed, and you will finally reign with my Son.

You will then see it was worth it to me to develop your true character and destiny From a Peasant, an out cast, who did not know who she is or what she could become, to my beautiful daughter, Kim for all to see My Princess who now walks in Victory!

Scriptures

Listed below you will find Bible scriptures that are categorized for your convenience. These scriptures may help you target your study to a specific area of concern. You will find as you walk in God's word and target your faith in prayer, that God will not only be faithful to his word but to you as well.

Abuse	Abandonment	Love/Loneliness
Hebrews 10:32-35	Matthew 28:20	John 14:1-3
Psalm 3:1-3	Psalm 50:15	Hebrews 13:5
Psalm 42:9	Isaiah 42:10	Joshua 1:5
Jeremiah 31:13	Psalm 121	John 16:32
Isaiah 60:10	Psalm 37:25	Psalm 23:4
Isaiah 62:21	John 4:10	John 3:16

Fear	Anger	Sexual Abuse
Ezekiel 28:26	Ephesians 4:26	Luke 13:11-12
Micah 7:5	Psalm 37:4	Philippians 3:12-14
Romans 2:9	Psalm 37:8	Romans 6:4
Psalm 18:1-3	Matthew 5:91	John 3:2
Proverbs 14:16	James 1:192	Corinthians 5:17
Psalm 56:11	Isaiah 26:3	Matthew 5:44

Shelter	Self-Esteem	Overcomer
Psalm 91:1-4	Proverbs 3:26	Isaiah 40:31
Psalm 23:1	Isaiah 30:15	Philippians 4:13
Psalm 37:25	2 Corinthians 2:71	John 5:4
Deuteronomy 26:15-19	Proverbs 28:1	Revelation 3:21
John 14:1-31	John 5:14	Revelation 3:12
Deuteronomy 28:11-12	Psalm 139:13-14	Psalm 40:2-3

NOTES

NOTES

NOTES

NOTES

Sources

Unless otherwise indicated, all scripture quotations are taken from the Holy Bible: King James Version. Copyright 1962. Used by permission of Zondervan Publishing House. The "King James Version" trademarks are registered in the Unites States Patent and Trademark Office by International Bible Society.

Citation: Huitt, W. (2004). Maslow's Hierarchy of Needs. Educational Psychological Interactive. Valdosta, GA: Valdosta State University. Retrieved July 2005 from: http://chiron.valdosta.edu/whuitt/col/regsys/maslow.html.

Webster's Dictionary - 1989 Edition; Based upon the lexicography of Noah Webster, LLD, Editor-in-Chief, Edward N. Teall, A.M. Lexicographer

U.S. Children's Bureau, (2005) AFCARS report #10. http://www.acf.hhs.gov/programs/cb/stats_research/afcars/tar/report 10.htm. Washington DC: U.S. Department of Health and Human Services (HHS)

Child Welfare League of America - Adoption and Foster Care Analysis and Report 2003

U.S. Children's Bureau, (2005). Child maltreatment 2003. Reports from the states to the National Child Abuse and Neglect Data System. http://www.acf.hhs.gov/programs/cb/pubs/cm03/index.htm

Contact Author

To correspond with Kim Hood, you may write to her:

        C/O Royalty Publications
        P.O. Box 132214
        Tyler, Texas 75713-2214

Email her at:
kimhood@peasanttoaprincess.com

Visit her website at: www.PeasanttoaPrincess.com

For information on booking her for a speaking engagement:
Call 1-877-221-6541

If you would you like to order
From a Peasant to a Princess
Please complete and mail the order form below. Make check or money order payable to E-BookTime, LLC.

From a Peasant to a Princess ISBN 1-59824-321-7

Copies ____   Price Each $8.95   Total _____
Alabama residents add 4% sales tax: _____
Shipping and handling: $5.95
                        Net Total   _____

___ Check or money order
___ Charge credit/debit card __ Visa __ Mastercard
Name on Card   _____
Billing Address _____
                 _____
         City   _____
         State ___ ZIP _____
Card Number   _____
Valid Through _____ / _____

Shipping Address if Different Than Billing Address
Name   _____
Address   _____
           _____
     City _____
     State ___ ZIP _____

Note: We cannot ship to P.O. boxes.
Delivery contact phone number _____

Send To   E-BookTime, LLC
               6598 Pumpkin Road
               Montgomery, AL 36108

(Price and availability subject to change.)

Printed in the United States
212815BV00001B/117/A